ANIMALS IN MY BACKYARD

ANIMAL BOOK 4 YEARS OLD

Children's Animal Books

BABY PROFESSOR
EDUCATION KIDS

Speedy Publishing LLC
40 E. Main St. #1156
Newark, DE 19711
www.speedypublishing.com
Copyright 2017

In this book, we're going to talk about animals you might see in your backyard. So, let's get right to it!

You don't have to go to a zoo to see animals. There are probably lots of animals in your backyard or in your neighborhood, especially at night when they come out to hunt.

Some of the animals can't hurt you but you should always be careful when you find an animal outdoors. Some of the larger animals do carry diseases so don't pick them up or touch them! Even if they look cute, they're not pets.

Northern Cardinal

BIRDS

If you have trees and shrubs in your backyard, then you'll probably have birds of all different types around. Birds are usually quite scared of people, but if you feed birds in your yard, after a while they are a little less afraid.

Some can get quite tame. If you like watching birds, you might want to get some binoculars so that you can see them more closely. Putting out different types of feeders with their favorite foods will attract them. Some types of birds might nest in your yard, too.

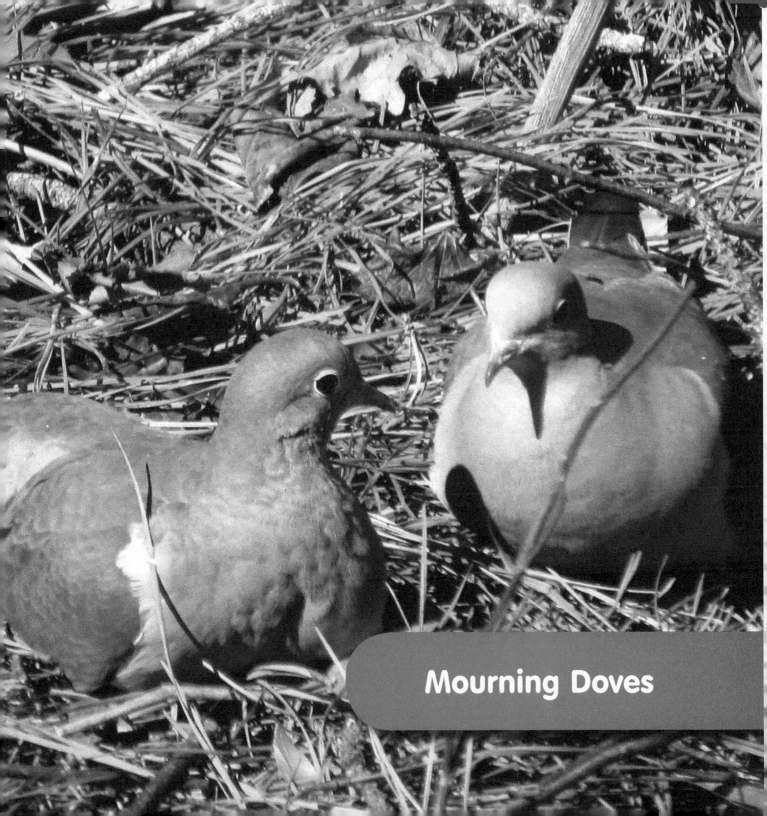

Mourning Doves

Hummingbird

Common backyard birds come in all different sizes and colors and they are fun to watch. Hummingbirds are the tiniest. They feed on the nectar from flowers just like butterflies. Most types of birds eat seeds, insects, and plants.

Small sparrows, wrens, and chickadees are types of birds you might see depending on where you live. Beautiful red cardinals, springtime robins, aggressive black crows, egg-stealing blue jays, and cooing turtle doves may be around as well. You might even see a big bird of prey like a hawk or an owl.

Blue jay

BUTTERFLIES

There are lots of different types of butterflies that you might see in your backyard. Around the world there are about 20,000 different types! Butterflies are insects with four beautiful wings that have bright colors and patterns.

Sometimes butterflies have markings that look like eyes on their wings. They eat nectar from flowers and they taste the nectar by using their feet. They fly from flower to flower in search of food. A butterfly starts life as a tiny egg no bigger than the period at the end of this sentence. When it hatches, it is a very hungry caterpillar. Eventually, it builds a chrysalis and goes through an amazing change.

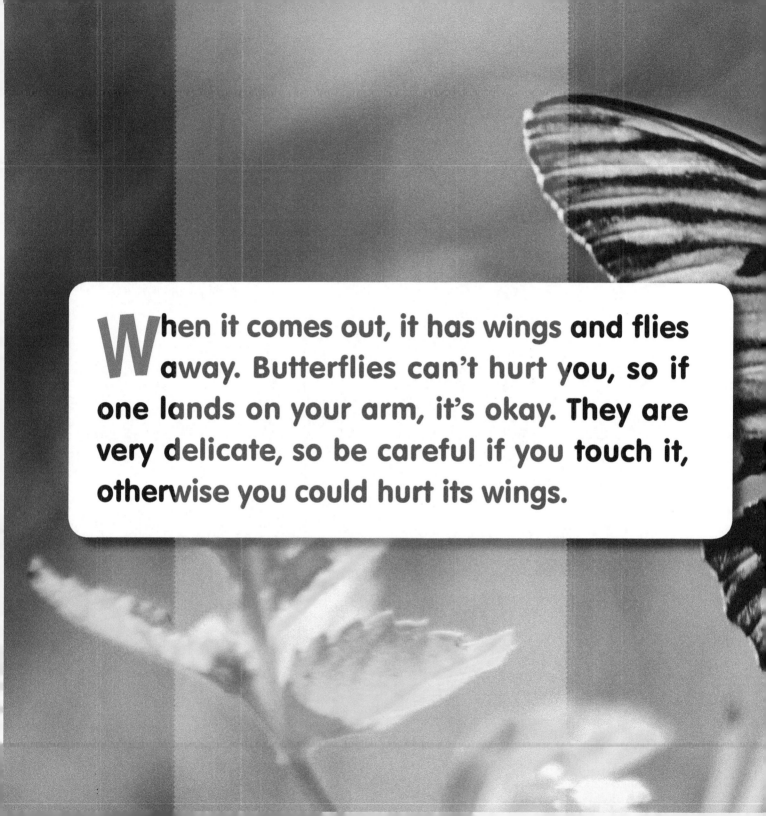

When it comes out, it has wings **and flies away**. Butterflies can't hurt **you**, so if one lands on your arm, it's okay. They are very delicate, so be careful if you **touch it,** other**wise you could hurt its wings.**

DEER

If you live near a wooded area, you might see deer. Deer are plant-eating mammals with four legs and a tail. They have an even number of toes on their hooves. They usually live in forests or grasslands. Sometimes deer come into backyards because they like to eat plants and flowers.

Some people don't like to have deer in their yards for that reason. Baby deer are called fawns. Fawns have white spots until they get older. A female deer is called a doe and a male deer is called a buck. The males have large antlers on their heads. Males use their antlers when they fight.

Mountain Lion

Deer have been hunted by men for thousands of years. They have lots of predators, which simply means that lots of animals, like mountain lions, like to eat them. When deer are scared, they run away in a zig zag pattern so other animals can't catch them. It's harder to shoot an animal that runs this way too.

FROGS AND TOADS

If you have a pond in your backyard, chances are likely that you'll see some frogs or toads. Both frogs and toads are types of amphibians. Frogs have longer legs than toads. A frog's skin is smoother than a toad's is. Toads have thick, bumpy skin and live mostly on land.

Frogs live mostly in the water and have webbed feet. Both frogs and toads are good for backyard gardens. They eat slugs and other pest insects. They eat lots of flies and mosquitoes that can carry disease.

If you have a cat or dog that plays **outdoors** you should try to keep them away **from these** amphibians. Usually, frogs and toads **can run** away from household pets, but **sometimes** they get caught and killed. Some **types of** frogs and toads are poisonous to pets as well.

RABBITS

If you have a grassy area in your yard, it wouldn't be surprising to find a rabbit nibbling on a piece of grass there. Rabbits are mammals with long ears, powerful back legs, and puffy tails that look like balls of cotton.

A wild rabbit in your backyard will **look a lot different** than a pet rabbit doe**s. Rabbits** are very shy and will generally run away if you get close to them.

Many people don't like rabbit**s in their** yards, because they cause damage **to plants.** They also poop a lot! Rabbits can **munch up** vegetable gardens and flowers in **the spring.**

They eat bark and shrubs in the winter. Rabbits are known for having babies very quickly so you might find a nest of rabbits in a grassy area. Baby rabbits leave their nests when they're about three weeks old.

RACCOONS

Raccoons look like little bandits and they love mischief. They are fuzzy with markings on their faces that look like black masks. They're cute, but remember they're wild animals. Sometimes they can get angry and attack, if humans come close.

They also carry diseases like rabies so it's okay to watch them from a distance, but don't get near them. Raccoons can be found in both North and Central America. They also live in Europe and Japan.

Like red foxes, they have learned to live around humans. They like to live in hollow trees, but they'll also set up dens in barns or under houses. Raccoons are omnivorous, which just means they eat both meat and plants.

They love eggs too. They have adapted to city areas and will steal pet food and raid garbage cans to find food. If you have a dog door, they can get into your house.

RED FOXES

In many parts of the world, red foxes live near cities now. The reason is that these foxes have learned to live near people. They eat pet food or other food we leave around. They also eat field mice, squirrels, and other small backyard animals including insects. Don't leave your pet kitten or pet rabbit outdoors because foxes like to eat these animals.

Red foxes are smart as well as beautiful. They are the size of a small dog. They are fun to watch because they do clever things and they're fast. They have 28 different types of sounds to "talk" to other foxes.

SKUNKS

Skunks come out at night and there's a good chance that you might smell them before you see them. They are black and white mammals with furry tails. Skunks use glands in their rear ends to let out a bad-smelling spray to defend themselves. You definitely don't want to get near a skunk! Their spray can really hurt your eyes and their smell is awful.

Skunks only spray if they feel that they are threatened and can't escape. They usually stomp their front feet or twist their rear ends around before letting out their spray. If you come across a skunk, it's a good idea to walk away quietly and slowly so you can avoid getting sprayed.

SNAKES

If you see a snake in your garden, don't try to get rid of it or kill it. Some types of snakes are harmless and others are very dangerous. The best thing to do is walk away from it and keep your pets away from it too. Most people get bitten by snakes when they try to remove them from their backyards. In most cases, snakes don't like to be near people any more than people like to be around snakes!

SQUIRRELS

After birds, the animals that people watch in backyards the most are squirrels. Squirrels are mammals and a type of rodent related to chipmunks, mice, and rats. Unlike most other rodents, squirrels are more active during the day than at night.

Squirrels are very intelligent and acrobatic. They can walk on or hang from clotheslines and telephone wires. They run up and down trees and jump from branch to branch.

Some people don't like squirrels in their yards because they can sometimes eat baby birds and munch up food that's meant for songbirds.

Even though they cause trouble, **squirrels are** cute with their pointy ears, **big dark eyes,** and bushy tails. You can train **squirrels** to eat out of your hand, but make **sure you** ask your Mom and Dad if it's okay **first, since they** have sharp claws.

Awesome! Now you know more about all the different animals you might find right in your own backyard. You can find more Animal books from Baby Professor by searching the website of your favorite book retailer.

Visit

BABY PROFESSOR
EDUCATION KIDS

www.BabyProfessorBooks.com

to download Free Baby Professor eBooks
and view our catalog of new and exciting
Children's Books

CPSIA information can be obtained
at www.ICGtesting.com
Printed in the USA
BVHW010217040222
628063BV00016B/221

9 781541 910973